Tales *of* Socks *and* Splendour

Kevin Barron

First published in 2014

Illustrations by Kevin Barron

ISBN 978-0-473-37989-6 (Softcover)
ISBN 978-0-473-37990-2 (ePub)
ISBN 978-0-473-37991-9 (Kindle)
ISBN 978-0-473-37992-6 (eBook)

5

To Peter,
the most unlikely muse

Contents

Foreword

By Professor Lofty Gushing, Shuffield University

It has been many years since the "foul-bummed" Grumpete and his glamorous partner the Kazza Princess first entered the canon of English literature. Their arrival came like a pork medallion to a meat eater at a vegetarian banquet: a surprise, yet no less welcome for it.

Over the years, they have had adventures involving, amongst other things, exploding volcanoes, carnivorous hedges and a sweet-eating nightingale. All these are collected in this volume, together with new adventures as exciting and entertaining as any which have gone before.

Yet it is not simply their escapades which please the reader. These are but the bait to lure him in. Closer attention to the text reveals far more. Themes emerge such as loyalty and reward, the benefits to the soul of a healthy life, the mortality of man in the face of the power of universe, the beguiling and often serendipitous nature of chance and the liberation from class constraints through worthy action. All these and more offer the reader even greater nourishment than the dishes on the metaphorical dessert tray would seem at first glance to be offering, and new flavours can be discovered on every tasting.

The style has changed little over the years with nods to Edward Lear, Douglas Adams and the great Lewis Carroll. The verse whips the reader along and, in its mesmeric frenzy, convinces him that all the words he is reading are real while at the same time, allowing no small amount of amusement at the sparkle of the vocabulary.

A mystery has remained at the heart of these poems which many eminent academics, the author of this Foreword included, have attempted to solve. What are the true identities of the Grumpete and the Kazza Princess themselves?

Hundreds of pages of analysis of references in the text, which even an amateur reader can see must be inspired by reality, have been undertaken, but all have failed to correlate their findings convincingly with any individuals living or dead. For the author of this Foreword, this delicious mystery serves only to enhance the enjoyment of these works.

With the collection of all the poems into a single volume, enchantingly illustrated by the author himself, the literary world is left to wonder whether it signals that a curtain has been drawn on the Grumpete's adventures. Only time will tell, but for my part, I believe there is hope still for those of us who love to lose ourselves in the world of the Ocean of Spleg and the Mountains of Torm.

I will delay you no further from entering this magical world. The poems await you. Bon voyage!

The Poems

The Ballad of the Grumpete and the Kazza Princess

Over the Ocean of Spleg and the Mountains of Torm,
Where the rain rarely rains and the sun's seldom shone,
The Grumpete he plodded, he heaved and he rolled,
With his bagful of socks and his socks full of mould,
Til he came to a land of a wide vastity
With its ears in the clouds and its toes in the sea.

And there on the shore, was a castle of height
Where the Grumpete fell down at the marvellous sight
Of the turrets all curled and the walls made of bone
And the Kazza Princess who lived there all alone.

He set down his bag at the tremulous gate
And tucked in his socks so as not to be late.
Then into those halls he lurched and he sprang,
While off mighty mirrors his whistled march rang.

And deep, deep inside in a kitchen of chrome,
The Kazza Princess had made there her home.

Her bowls were like jewels with faceted faces,
Her spoons and her forks bent in all the right places.

Her towels of pink suede hung on witchety hooks
Below the shelf bowing down with the old comic books.
And a nightingale sat on the microwave's top,
With a mint in its mouth and its hat like a mop.

Under gloomery arches a strange path was laid:
The crummy damp patches his bootless feet made
As the galumphing Grumpete wund his wearisome way,
While the day turned to night and the night turned to day.

Down the high chimbley chimney the sun slid a finger;
It wormed down the bricks, it seeped over the cinder,
And tapped on the heel of the Kazza Princess
Who was nearly awake, or awake more or less.

At the thin line of dawn, she stifled a yawn,

While the ploffing of feet stroked the cheek of the morn.

Then there in the doorway, with arms long and hairy,

Was a whiskersome bladder, in no way a fairy,

Who chuckled a chuck and gibbered his gut,

Then pulled out a stool and rested his butt,

While from out of the shadows, the Kazza Princess

Surveyed of his jawbone and his brain in recess.

And sudden the sun fell out of its bed.

Startled light tumbled downwards, through window it

sped

And filled all the chrome with a dazzling bright

And the Grumpeter's eyes with an awesomeful sight,

For the Kazza Princess sat with deep dark brown eyes

And long nylon sparkly, silvery thighs.

With a belch and a fart the Grumpete stood up straight

And picked from beside him the fullest of plates

And stuffed it all in with a pleased lack of style.

'Twas something the Kazz had not seen for a while.

But she'd heard of these things in the stories of old:

Of odiferous satchels, of socks and of mould.

So she tried out a smile she picked up off a tray

And found it fit well and inclined there to stay.

So the days they wound on, round the spool of the year.

Dark clouds grew up tall and the rains fell quite near.

And the waters arose and ran through the gate

So the Grumpeter unhitched an octagonal plate.

And on it they piled all the socks they could find,

And the nightingale too, for it hadn't yet dined.

Then they sailed through a window down dellies of green,

The unlikeliest of crews in that land ever seen:

A gargling Grumpete and a kimmering Kazz

And a mint-sucking songbird who was one of the lads.

They shipped through the mountains to the Ocean of

Spleg,

Where the Kazza Princess trailed a silvery leg,

And the Grumpete picked up a sock by the heel.

Added garlic and mustard and created a meal.

Then splashing and rolling and picnicking thus,

They travelled the waves and were picked up by a bus

Which set them right down on the welcoming strand

Of the Grumpete's precipitous, ferny home land.

Now over the hillocks they jolly and jape;

The Kazza Princess and her sock-eating ape.

The Grumpete and Kazza Princess
meet the volcano

If you fell through the cloudtops, slid down the rain,

If you got caught on a thermal and sent up again,

If you bounced and you rolled through the thickening air,

If you dodged chatty seagulls who'd stop talking and stare,

If your knees scraped on mountains and your clothes
caught on ice,

If you caught sight of wide vistas beyond any price,

If you were mazed in a chaos of fuzzing and scree,

There's only one place you could jolly well be,

And that's in the land where the epitrolls meet,

The home of the crumb-belching foul-bummed
Grumpete.

Come, skoot up the valley, go whisk through the grass,

Skirt the old forest and pass through the pass,

Wend on through the tussocks which grow oh so high,

Tread lightly through boglings 'til on to the dry,

And up mongst the bouldery mossery rocks,

You'll find a large Healthy Life Biscuit crate box.

Two doors and four windows, curtains and old vests,
And curled in the corner, the Kazza Princess.

With a bart and a furp and a brackly jaw,
The Grumpete stood up and leaned his legs by the door,
And gazed over mountains, where clouds met the stone,
And the Kazza looked too, so he wasn't alone.
Then over the wildness they spied distant smoke
Curling up like a cotton reel around an old spoke.

So without much aword, they lifted their packs,
Took ice axe from fridge and spare ears made of wax,
Pulled on all their boots made of epitroll leather,
Which were especially adapted to be worn together,
They whipped on their mittens and pulled on their hats,
Smearing over their bodies a cream made from fats
Of the six-legged sheepies which dwold thereabouts,
For protection from cold and from hot and from gout.
Then skipping and hopping and lurching along,
They both wandered off doing a gargling song
Which they learnt from a drainpipe one blastery night
As they huddled together round the roaring firelight.

Many days they walked on over fields, under stiles,

In mud to their eyeballs, they sludged many miles,

But always aware with beanies up top,

They could follow each other's wool bobbly-bob.

Scrambling cliff faces, looking into the sky,

Ever nearer and closer, the smoke winding high,

Which sooner became a thick, dark, lofty pall,

Billowing, sinking and spreading out tall,

Until it had munched up the clouds from the blue,

Then gazed on with hunger and ate that up too.

Til the whole world seemed crammed with a smoggit so

dense,

That our heroes decided to put up their tents.

There was one for them both and the other for the feet

Of the sock-rotting, shoe-slaying, grubby Grumpete.

And that night by the tent-flap, enticing the kettle

To boil on a guano-warmed plate of hot metal,

They saw in the sky an orangey glow

Which shone on the smok lighting it from below;

A flickering, eerie old reddening sight,

Like a couple of traffic lights having a fight,

While below them a mountain loomed conical strange,

Its dark brooding character looked awfully dange.

So up it next morning, they shouldered their bags,

Climbing bent double, like a couple of hags.

They pickled their way through dense shrubbery.

Then came a loud bang, legs went rubbery,

As the once firm ground shook, smoke poured 'cross the

sky,

And yea eftsoons eke, they thought they might die.

But it wearied away so they trudged up and on,

And the Grumpete he whistled his old marching song.

As up they ascended, all scending on up,

The Grumpete munched steadily a jelly-filled bap.

Then the Kazza Princess saw the plants die away,

And the thick hanging smoke made a night of the day,

While the soil underfoot became blackened and dust;

For those into deserts it was surely a must.

For e'er and about was there nowt to be seen,

Not a libbo of life, not a spillit of green.

But instead all was desert and barren and waste:

It wasn't the place you would run to in haste.

Many thousands of feet they walked up to the cloud,

Which was smurky and dirty and far too damn loud

For normal grey clouds or dark thunderheads

Which terrify you down to the foot of your bed.

They rained bits of grit, some all aglow,

Fried chitlins and smatlins bounced down to and fro.

Then the land levelled out and they came close to a hole,

A huge and steep-sided and hellish type bowl;

The gate to old Hades, the way to the Pit;

It made them so jolly scared they were both nearly sick.

But they pulled them together with special long string

Which was wondrously strong and tinily thin.

Then they peered over the edge and into the seeth

That was bubbling and churning and boiling beneath,

All achurn and aplop and aburning and pus,

And worst of all, they'd no getaway bus.

A mighty loud belch and eructation of gases

Made the Grumpete turn green on his envious chassis,

While out from the depths came a geyser so dire,

Pulling debris and flame from the horrible mire.

It leapt up to greet them without shaking hands,

Spilling both over backwards and choking their glands,

Sweeping down the long slope on a torrent of lava,

You never in your life saw such a palaver!

Protected from heat by the sheepie fat cream,

Kazz hoiked out the ice-axe and then like a dream,

She flung it attached to a rope jolly long

Through a cloud of yellowy, sulphurous pong.

The Grumpete, now greener, saw that it fell

In the ground by a rock on the clear side of Hell.

With a twist of her body, the Kazz threw her legs

Round his waist in a firm grip - um - a question now begs:

For the fat cream protected their bodies from fire,

But their clothes would be burnt off, or wilt call me a liar?

And indeed as she dragged their way out of the flood,

At last they were safe, but both now in the nud.

Once out of the way, they surveyed of the wreck

Of themselves and their luggage, but oh what the heck:

The land it was desolate, lonesome and broad,

If they couldn't get home unseen, then, well, nobody

could.

So with axe o'er one shoulder and rope round a knee,

Grumpete and Princess set off back home for tea.

And sud there before them, there stretched out a road,

(Embarrassed map-reader the Grumpete's face glowed).

So the naked parade marched easier,

Of the two walkers there, the Grump greasier.

Then round a far bend without any fuss

Came a big red and white striped and tourist-filled bus!

Emptying its contents there out of its side,

From cameras and flashguns there was nowhere to hide,

For the road it was wide and the fields they were flat

Our friends had no clothes on, not even a hat.

So heads held up high and axe at the waist,

Through a crowd of the curious our fearless friends paced.

Of all of their bottoms was gotten a peek...

I'd better not tell you, it would be a cheek.

But ever on photos all over the world,

One hairy old bottom, one tastefully curled.

At last and at last and at last and at last,

By a short-cut, a rope bridge and walking quite fast,

They came to their dwelling, a good sight to see,

Where the Grump broke the door for he'd losted the key.

The Grumpete and the Kazza Princess get lost

The Grump and the Kazz, you'll remember from yore,
Were a smell and a glam from another far shore,
But 'tho oft they'd adventured around and about
From eating their socks, they'd become somewhat stout.

So once of a morn they shouldered their guts
And set off quite fast through the gilbery wutts
Until they lost sight of their home far below,
For there in the clouds it had started to snow.

They walked and they crawled, they climbed and they ran
And they tried to lose fat just as fast as they can,
But their legs they were stiff and their muscles aflab
So their performance was, well, quite honestly - shab.

Til fanting and parting and ached at the knees,
They collapsed feeling sicky with armpits like cheese.

And the Kazza Princess looked around and she said

How much things were different from just lying in bed,

For once they'd been fit and galumphed all the day

Round the mounts and the dips and gone swum in the
bay.

But now things had changed and there wasn't the time

Or the feeling or incline or far too much wine

And they'd packed up their packles and mothballed their
feet

And focused on sock dishes, savoury and sweet,

Til the Grumpete grew expert and tried writing a book

And took it to Kazz so she could have a look.

But not a line or a squig could she really make out,

For the Grump had no pen and had gone and used trout

Whose ink, as you know, is watery thin

And the recipe sock was consigned to the bin.

So on in this way all corrupted and sloth,

The pair had got fat and to get up were they loath.

Til this time when we find them all down in the scree

Trying to get fit, but just thinking of tea.

And the Kazza she thought of a huge lump of choc
And how in the choc shop round the boxes she'd flock
And grab it in handfuls and giggle and scoff
And wipe off her hands on a silvery cloth.
Til contented and smudged around at the lips
She'd stagger on homeward with her hands on her hips,
Cos it made other people think she was in charge
And not a princess with a chocappetite large.

Meanwhile the Grumpete, the sweaty old swell,
Would play in the kitchen, which made quite a smell,
But he'd mop it all up with a sock from his bag
And hang it outside before using the scrag
From the toe to flavour his pots
In flavours quite ripe which would tie up in knots
Any gullet or stomach which wanted to see
Just what culinary delights the Grumpete ate for tea.
For he had an intestine of carbonised steel
And could eat anything for his monstrous type meal.
And even the Kazz could now find the feet
For meals which once made her go white as a sheet.

So daydreaming, food-wishing and exhaustified thus,

They wondered if maybe they should refurbish the bus

That had brought them so far over land and by sea

To the place where they finally had settled to be.

But that seemed too much work for the bus it was old,

It would have to be something which was much more
bold.

They picked themselves up and looked round at the snow

And wondered then which direction to go.

For the cloud it was thick and their knowledge was gone

Of the direction they'd come and got up that place from.

They hummed and they harred and they scratched of their
bonce

For of the way down they hadn't a nonce.

Til at last the Grumpete with impeccable style

Let rip of a gust which lasted a while.

Then off did he set in a direction which seemed

Remarkably sensible, at least that's what he deemed.

And the Kazza, just noticing, set off at a trot,

Making sure to keep clear of his thundering bot

Which let off its charges with an astonishing roar
And left her still wondering what he did it for.

Still on they galumphed, til slowing down knacked,
They'd not got this direction thing any near cracked,
For they couldn't see anything familiar in the fog,
Not a rock or a bun or a bush or a log.
But they carried right on, still hoping to find
A path or a sight which would call to their mind
The memory of somewhere they'd seen on the way out,
So they searched all around and about and about.
But nothing of cognise sprung to their glance -
For all that they knew they'd gone wandered to France.
So onward for hours they limpled and hobbed,
A-chewing on berries they pressed in their gobs

In an attempt to assuage the hungering pangs

That tore at their tummies with very sharp fangs.

And the day it grew dark as the night came upon,

And the Kazza did frown for the day it was gone

And her pathfinder was grumpy cos he hadn't a map

Which now he had realised was rather mishap.

So arguing both on the desolate moor,

They calmed down enough in their arms for to snore.

The night it was cold and the snow and the frost

Tugged at the souls of the benighted and lost.

The next day it dawned damp and chill and sore grim,

But still where lay home, they hadn't a whim.

So onward they journeyed deep into the wild

And scrambled 'mongst boulders which bout them were

piled.

And as the second day drew to another dark close,

The Kazz sadly sat down and blew loud on her nose

For another cold night was beckoning still

And frankly the last had been somewhat chill.

The Grumpete lumbered over and patted her head

And promised her then a warm cosy bed.

And off he did set of agathering fern,

And branches and twigs and things for to burn.

And rustling and panting and carrying lots

He whipped out a penknife and a handful of knots.

These he did ply with a skill to admire

And soon he had built, cripes not only a fire,

But a double skinned tent which was full sleeping bagged

And a hot water tank which was wonderfully lagged.

So out of the elements they snuggled the night

And the frost tried in vain at their tootsies to bite.

So when morning came all they lacked was some food

But Kazz didn't ask him for that would have been rude.

So she decided her job for the day had to be

To find something nice they could have for their tea.

She collected some berries and pulled up some roots

And plucked from some branches some tender young

                                        shoots

And added some snow and a wild herb or five,

Til she'd brewed up a stew that made them feel alive.

And the days turned to weeks and the weeks turned to
more,

And still were they lost in the fog on the moor.

Til one day it cleared and they walked to the edge

And saw far below them their own garden hedge.

So tumbling, rolling and jollicking down,

They arrived at their abode as happy as clowns.

And they looked at each other as they got to the door

At changes which somehow they'd not noticed before.

For the weeks of tough hardship and diet and toil

Had wreaked a revenge on their mortal coil

And where once had been flab with a dullness of sheen

Was finely toned muscle which wasn't half lean.

So grinning and happy the two celebrate

On the funny old things that can happen with fate.

And to prepare for a meal, the Grumpete delved in his
box

And pulled out for dinner his very best socks.

The marriage of the Grumpete and the Kazza Princess

Tis many a year since lasted we speak,

Of the Kazza Princess and the foul-bummed Grumpete,

Who had set up a cottage of Healthy Life Bisk

Which for a dainty like Kazz was not short of risk.

But she was prepared for her paramour true,

Despite of his socks, which smelled just like poo,

For love had she found, if you could call it that

Which you find wearing one day not unlike a hat

Which falls from the sky, without hardly a word,

And your sense of reality becomes somewhat blurred,

Which in the land where they dwell is rather surprising

For normality there is hid in disguising.

For realness to blur could be rather scary

And that's saying much when you live with a hairy

Great fellow with a jaw that was once used to lift

A massive great boulder which the bold couldn't shift.

For that was a favour the Grumpete had done once

For a neighbouring chap who was kind of a dunce,

Since he'd ask for the rock shop to drop at his door

A bloody great rock, don't ask me why for.

And once it was there, right much he had puzzled

And scratched of his bonce and rubbed at his muzzle.

Until it occurred to his ponders to wonder

If the Grump and his chin could perform a wonder.

And surely they did, for they are quite a team,

Of certain the best the Kazz she had seen.

'Twas one of the charms that had caught her off guard,

That and the things he could sculpt out of lard

Which showeded to her his more sensitive side,

Which to most of the world was a thing he did hide.

For he was as humble as the smallest of shrub,

Except if you got between him and his grub.

So one day, of sudden and out of the blue

Which arose like a fog from a puddle of spew

Which someone (the Grump?) had left lie on the ground,

And had brought up all quiet with nary a sound,

The Grump took it on him to bend of his knee

And mutter some words. Could they be "Marry me"?

The Kazz kind of stopped, she still can recall it,

Saying "Do please ask again when I'm out of the toilet,

And please close the door behind as you go

So that the whole of my doings to the street doesn't show,

For it sure wouldn't do for a princess like me

On the toilet by commoners and others to see.

But for you, dear Grump, I'll make an exception

For I've always had plans for a wedding reception."

Not much long later she'd done with her wiping

And the delayified Grump had stopped of his griping,

The Kazza Princess stood tall near the cellar

And the sock-eating Grump touched ground to patella

And doffed of his hat, which was new made of fluff

Which had once been the cats' til they'd haded enough

And had brushed it all out til they were shiny and new

And could proudly and grandly utter the mew

Which meant "Look we've licked ourselves clean as a

whistle

And brushed of our fur on a brush made of thistle

Which has long handy thorns to massage our coat

And can of course tickle our delicate throat."

So he doffed of his cap and shuffled his feet,

For losted for words was the once brave Grumpete,

For she looked tall and grand and he felt like the dregs

In front of those great big long silvery legs.

Yet she smiled kindly on, for she knew she was dazzling,

But this helped him not for his heart she was frazzling.

And he muttered and stuttered and twisted around

His hat which screeched with a caticular sound.

For sure it had happened that he'd mistakenly taken

One cat for a hat so his hat was a fake'un.

The shock of the screech pushed the fear of his question

Out the way, cos two fears would give fear indigestion.

And out like a madrigal, clear and serene

Came those loveliest of words in this pome ever seen.

"Oh Kazza Princess, oh Queen of us we,

Please do me the honour to marry of me."

And a tear she let fall, which he caught on a spoon

Like a love-stricken, fond-footed, gibbering loon.

The tear made a ring which he put on her finger.

I think in this space, we musn't long linger

For there's much to be told of the day they were wed

And many the tear that the audience shed

As the vows were exchanged on slabs of brown bread

Which with peanut butter were thoughtfully spread

So the vows they would stick and never fall off

No matter how much the family might cough.

For once it was thought that the Kazz had self lowered

For her Grumpete so foul, while her family had glowered.

For they felt he was common and not one to be

Associate with their mob, who were royalty.

But accept him they did, for they realised with a start

That the Kazza had made him the king of her heart.

The celebrations started with the traditional fire

Where all of the cakes were thrown onto the pyre.

'Twas a royal tradition which the Grump felt was wasting

The greatest of cakes which he should have been tasting.

When no one was looking, that resourceful bloke

Made use of distractions and dived into the smoke

And pulled out the feast and stuffed all in his socks.

Believe me on those there are no need of locks.

For brave would he be the man who went close to

Those parts which riot police once took a hose to,

For they thought a rabble was coming right up the street

When 'twas really the sound of the smell of his feet

Which can be disturbing if you aren't used to feeling

Your grip on your senses is suddenly reeling.

So the cake it was saved for a late midnight feast

And it proved a good job, for 'twas not to be missed.

And after the fireworks and honeymoon on

A luxury bus cruise round the Swampers of Flon,

The pair settled down in the cottage once more

Where the sea and the mountains are seen from the door,

And did of those things which if there ain't no abating

End up with the Kazz and Grump proliferating.

One day she woke up and found under her jumper

A bloomin' great blob which would kick her and thump

her.

And the Grumpete let out an almighty "Hurrah!"

While the Kazz did a much more dainty "Tra la!"

So the days turned to months and before that to weeks

For rhyming with months requires this sort of tweaks.

Til all of the world seemed to be in on the wait,

Oh how unoriginal to be somewhat late.

Until came the time when the shrimp started to fumble

And many hours later came out with a tumble.

He looked around calm at his parents' bright faces

And of previous home dusted off of the traces.

He asked for his dinner and stretched out his hand

Like the newborn can do on his own new found land.

So that dear listener you'll believe is a truey,

How world saw first our new hero, King Louis.

King Louis the Hedgehunter

It's one of the mysteries of now and to be
How a chap can grow up from the size of a pea
And part of that tale of the world, it is true,
Is how the Grumpete must have once grew and grew.
For it's hard to believe how that monstrous great lump
Could ever have been just the tiniest of bump.
But what happened betwixt and between those two times
Is not a fit subject to be met by these lines.

For this is about a quite different fellow,
The one whose appearance was met with a bellow
Of joy like a belch been combined with a cannon
Which was fired over hillside and mountain and on in
To the night and beyond, for this was Grump's firstborn
Which had tumbled out onto the veg of their lawn.

And the Kazza Princess was certainly jaded
Right down to her silvery legs which had faded.
But right quick and real soon she got back her vigour
While the Grumpete had said he thought he'd be bigger.

She just rolled of her eyes and tutted her head

And took King Louis back to his bed.

For that was his name, for his Ma she had felt

That it would mean she could buy him a majestical belt

Which was gilded with felspar and embossed with snails

And hung all about with some madrigal's tails.

The Kazz was a princess so it's fair clear to me

That *King* Louis is natural as natural can be.

The Lou flapped his ears and his fingers he flexed

And did a slight frown like you'd think he was vexed,

Where in fact he exercose his magical powers,

Which flowed from his fingers like scent flows from

                                                    flowers.

He used of his magic for distracting you

From his nethers which meanwhile were pouring out poo.

For it's a truth true to tell and verily so,

That if stuff comes in one end out the oth it must go.

But back to the magical stuff with his hands,

A rare skill to have e'en in these weirdy lands.

But with dextrous wavings and hexifous fuss

He could jiggle his fingers for example thus…

And all those around would gasply say "Oh"

For I think you'd agree twas a wonderful show.

But he grew and he fed and slept once or twice

And gazed much at ceilings and wandering wood lice.

And the Grumpete he nuzzled and cooed, it was odd

How he patted the noggin and tickled his gob.

Meanwhile the Princess formed out of her hair

An intricate basket which made up the lair

Of our hero minute but less so each day,

For his bod was expanding the usual way

That relates to the mystery I mentioned before

Of growth and potential and you can be sure

That before time moves on - and it already has -

He'll grow a bit more while listening to jazz.

For the parentals had heard that some sorts of music

Can be for your child somewhat quite therapeutic.

So jazz and baroque was all you could hear

If beside of their cottage you happened to near.

One day when the wind blew off from the sea

And the sun came from sky and peeked round a tree,

The Grump and the Kazz decided to go

All the hills and the fields to King Louis to show.

So they packed him all up in his little suit red

And the Grump balanced him on the top of his head.

Young Louis he slept and dangled his feet

Into Grumpeter's eyes and his eyebrows so neat.

For fatherhood made him to scrub up his looks

And he'd fashioned his brows in a style got from books.

Up into the hills the twain plus one more

Went walking and talking with sometimes a snore.

But on top of the hill they halted their step

And down from the Grumpete the little chap lep

And hands on his hips he did a survey

Of the world down below which all around lay.

And what did he see but a myriad fields

All scattered and quilted and producing forth yields,

As is the job of the fields thereabouts

Whether sheepies or cattle or carrots or sprouts.

It concerned him much that all was surrounded

By nasty great hedges, it made him to frowneded.

For they bristled with briars and twittered with twigs,
They prickled and bustled and even ate pigs.

One went just then as it thrust forth his nose
And was gobbled all up not leaving its toes.
It was quite a shock for our hero so small
For nothing to him bad happened at all
All cocooned in his hair bed, protected by socks
Which were as good a defence as learning to box.

That was the latest of tricks the Grumpete had found
For using his socks as a kind of guard hound.
No monster or fiend would dream of disturbing
A house permeated by smell so perturbing.

Louis turned to them both and looked quite upset
But received just a smile and a "What's up poppet?"
"Can't you see what's going on?" is what he wanted to say,
But as yet was too small to be talking that way
And out of his mouth came only saliva
Which the Kazz wiped off on the Grump's balaclava.
"The hedges are coming!" tried again little Lou
And trieded so hard that he squeezed out a poo.

But all that he got for his pains was a nappy
Provided by Ma and put on by his Pappy.

So muchly disgruntled with parents so thick
He bawled the way home til he made himself sick.
No matter how they tried to quiet him down,
He'd sit in his chair and whinge on and frown.
Couldn't they understand they had just been invaded
By bushranging hedges which throughout the fields raided?
All they would do though was pat him and feed him
It was mighty frustrating to have guardians so damn dim.

Once it was dark they put him into his room
And tried to persuade him to fall into a swoon,
But all he could think of was the fiendish foul foliage
Which even right now did plunder and pilliage.
Still his cries they were left quite all uninheeded,
But Louis himself knew now just what was needed.

When all were asleep he climbed from his cot
And out of the cupboard his red suit he got.
Then armed with bare hands and his hill tribesman's hat
He crept out of the house without waking the cat.

And out 'long the street he shouldered his arms
Trying before battle to stay somewhat calm.

And before you'd have known it he came to the edges
Of the terror struck fields surrounded by hedges.
A dramatic wind blew in off the sea
And young Louis wished then that he'd eaten more tea.
Torn clouds fled the sky and the moon was left naked
'Mongst the shivering stars which twinkled and shakéd.

Then out o'er the fields he began to stalk
And he was a professional; it was no time to talk.
For there in the distance was a hedgerow immense
All branches and twigs in a tangle so dense.

It stood feeding on field mice and chomping on shrews
Using flowers as salad which near it did grew.
King Lou had his quarry, that villainous growth,
And he would ne'er rest til he'd ripped out its throat.
From tussock to mud clod he dodged and he crept
Til out of the shadows his little form leapt.
The hedge was surprised and it started to leave
But the battle was on and it was no time to grieve

For the long days of summer and lascivious corn

It premonished sudden it would never see morn.

The duel it was fierce and it raged half the night.

Never before have you seen such a fight.

King Louis he dodged and he ducked and he dived.

He tried very hard and even he strived.

For the hedge it was fierce and the hedge it was strong

And the effort aroused from Lou's rear end a pong.

His father's own son he most surely was

And the hedge it was bushed and held of its nose.

Right then at that moment the King summoned his power

And from out of his fingertips tingled a shower

Of magic and hex and mystic and glitter

And the hedge shook its branches and became all ajitter.

Then it strangled and struggled and staggered and fell

And plunged down the abyss on the express straight to

hell.

And the King was exhausted and fell to the ground

Which was somewhat lumpy he annoyingly found.

So he picked himself up and set off back home

Loping with jaunt o'er the dampening loam.

And back in his bed he pondered his war

And felt it was probably worth shouting for.

So he let forth a cry of victory and cheer

If he'd been over eighteen, he'd've drunken a beer.

The more he thought on it, the better he felt

So he cheered and he shouted til his eyes 'gan to melt

For the first hard won victory is often the best

And from his undies rose up the sweet smell of success.

Finally his cheering was stopped on arrival

Of the grumpy Grumpete intent on survival

Til the fingers of dawn tugged open his eyes
Not the sounds of his son's bold victory cries.

"Shh little bugger, what the sock is the matter?
My ear drums you're socking well trying to shatter!"
He picked him up out of the Kazza hair soft
And to adulation of all was carried aloft.
At last, felt the Louis, he had founded the thing:
Of all of the hedgehunters, he sure was the King.

The Grumpete and Kazza
meet the Future Eater

It's been many moons, many stars, many socks,

Since Grumpete and the Kazz have unlocked their locks

And gone on adventures weirdy and bold

In the heat and the wind or the rain and the cold.

They'd spent all their time with the kith and the kin

But they'd done all that now and kith can wear thin.

They'd heaved and they'd harved on upbringing King
Louis

Through pustules and walking and underwear pooey,

Til now he stood tall with a great shock of hair

Which could only be cut by being stood on a chair.

But inside his gut Grump felt a great swell of rage,

Which gave vent to itself til his trousers were frayed,

That the time it had passed since the Kazz he'd first
wooed

With his musical bowel and sock footy stewed.

Those days had been fine and long in the telling,
Like the Princess's legs and the hair she put gel in.

As he looked at the stars from the door of their shack,
He decided that although he wanted nothing back,

It was time for a change and a flexing of feet
And he howled at the moon "I am the Grumpete!"
Til the Kazz raised herself from her comfortable chair
Where she reposed with a book in her lugubrious lair,
And asked of the Grump why he must make such noise
Which was louder than any much made by the boys
Who visited Lou in his foul pubey den
Where boys went to grow into foul pubey men.

He turned on his wife his teary stained eyes
And pulled from his nose a handful of flies
Which had rested themselves on one of his nosts
Without taking account of the fearfullest costs
Of precipitate acts on a Grumpeter's face
And their souls had took wing at such a quick pace
That their bodies had caught in the jungle of hair
Which grew from the sides of those nostrils to scare.

He flung the flies far and he gazed on the visage

Mounted in front of and above her long gizzage.

Twas the one he loved best and he knew she must come

On an adventure too under moon, stars or sun.

This he said with a burp to emphise his point

And underlined it further by cracking each joint.

The Kazza Princess looked up at a star

And watched as its light trickled down from afar,

And thought to herself, could it possibly be true

That the Grump had been pondering while not on the loo?

Then she took up his hand and said she would go

To wherever his heart and his feet bade him to.

So the creaking Grumpete shook out of his feet,

His arms and his legs and his back (quite a feat,

For twas padded with fat and with mould and with

crumbs

Which from eating while slouching inevitably comes).

Then he unhooked his pack from the back of the door

And filled it with socks, then a few more socks more

To eat on the way to wherever they went

And Kazz a gourmet-filled food tray ahead of her sent.

Then leaving a note for their gangling son
They lifted each foot and broke into a run
For the future was there at the end of the yard
And they wanted to grab it, not just read its card.

Once past the cabbage patch, each gave a leap
And landed in a mixed up Kazzgrumping heap
Outside of the lands where they'd chosen to stay
And were now both quite firmly astart on their way.

The road it stretched on til the edge of the sky
And they came to the edge of the land by and by,
Which was strange, they both thought, that they did really
                                              join
And not hover together like two sides of a coin.
So there looking round they rolled up the road
And the Grump rested not til in pack it was stowed,
For roads can be useful if treated quite right
And not tar-sealed and feathered in the mid of the night.

The Kazz leaned on the sky and rested her feet
On the place where the sky and the land usually meet,

And asked of the Grump what should they do then,

When out of the clouds came a fiery ahem.

And looking on up, they espied with afright

A frankly quite terrifying, scary old sight.

With leathery skin and a sad sagging jaw,

And its claws and dark wings all dripping in gore,

Was a creature of girth a-picking its teeth

And revealing the gold which lay underneath.

Through yellowing eyes it eyed-up the pair

And as afterthought added its most annoyed glare.

"What is it?" Grump cried. "Have I taken its road?"

Perhaps in response its eyes and teeth glowed.

Then clearing its throat with a delicate cough

The creature bowed twice and then gave a scoff.

"Roads I like not," it grarled through its jaws

Which, come to think of it, reminded of saws.

"I eat up the future and any road which there goes,

And that's why it's all ended without any throes.

And now it's your turn to be gobbled by me,

No last requests, it's time for my tea!"

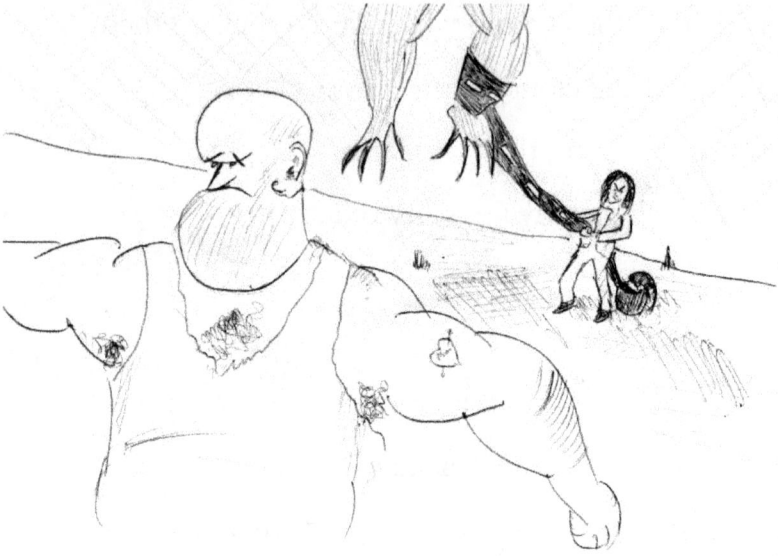

At that the Grump felt a familiar rage,

He had so very wanted to get off of this page,

Yet here on the sky was a bloody, grim ghoul

Which wanted their future as if by a rule.

It flapped of its wings and leapt from its perch

And the Kazza and Grump gave a quick sideways lurch

And dived to the ground to vacate the maw

Of the morrow-eating, gold toothed dinosaur.

With a screeching of anger it turned on a dime

And determined to get them this very next time.

But the Grump he was quick and he shook out his pack

And took a quick bite of a sock for a snack.

And the road it sprang out and the Kazz it did grab,

For she'd studied of knots in a knot-studying lab.

With a snap of the road she made a lasso

Which calmly she swung at the on-coming zoo.

The creature howled once, it howled twice and then thrice

And Kazz and Grumpete felt like tiny white mice

Caught in the gaze of a gigantic cat

With great teeth and claws and they didn't fancy that.

Its hot breath was hot and its leathery wings

Dropped scales and wet snot and unpleasant things

Which the Grumpete scooped up as he dived one more
time,

And pushed in his mouth with a basting of slime.

But the Kazz held her ground and whirled round her head

The Macadam rope the colour of lead

And snared as it dived, the foot of the beast,

Or that's what she thought it might be at the least.

It gave of a roar as it felt the snag

And the Kazz reached out for the Grumpete's old bag.

And picking it up she incited to run

The Grumpete's two legs and his feet and his bum.

The rest of him followed dragged on at the waist

While the beast it swerved round and angrily gave chase.

The road was unfurling and twisting about.

The Grumpete tried thinking again and gave shout,

For he'd seen that the future was opening up

Even now, for the creature had opened a gap.

So as it flew on dragging road by its toe,

The two knew they must follow wherever it go,

Til they could think of a way to escape its grasp.

Was this an adventure or a pain in the arsp?

There was no time to think for hot on their heels

Was a doomy hot breath each on their back feels.

It flapped, roared and squawked, it barked and it mooed,

Til the insides of both of their guts came unglued,

For fear lightens loads at times of distress

And this was indeed such a time, more or less.

So chased both by beast and by beastly smell,

The two they ran on, distinctly pell-mell.

It gained on them sure, though the road did unroll,

For every sole on the road it protected their soul.

Now the flapping was closer and their lungs were aheave;

They were both out of shape like you wouldn't believe.

And just at that moment when all had seemed lost,

From out of the night like an avenging ghost.

The Kazza's on-sent dinner tray shot into view

And into the mouth of the creature it flew.

The parameters here I will lay out for sure,

They are closing speed, weight of the food and one more:

The sharp edge of the tray which was designed as a knife

To cut up the food – she was a resourceful wife.

So the fast food supplies on the culinary blade

Connected so hard that you would need a spade

To collect all the bits of the grotesquery

Which had threatened them both with life's last mystery.

Of the meal there was nowt for the Kazza to eat.

All had vapourised, so ended her treat.

But the Grump was gallant and as husband was true,

He did what any Grumpeter would do.

He picked out his favourite rottingest sock

And offered it all, heel, toe, lock and stock.

The Kazza she sighed, she'd never got the taste,

But it seemed now she hung-panged too good to waste.

So she took it with thanks and swallowed it down

And almost quite managed to disguise her frown.

The Grumpete looked as smug as a cat full of cream:

Watching Kazz eating socks had been his always dream.

Then once more hand in hand down the road they went

nifty,

To make what they could of the next years of fifty.

The Grumpete in the kitchen

When the rain it is raining and it rains all the time,

And there's little to do except drink too much wine,

But the wine is too red or too wet or too dry,

And you've had so much now that you think you could

cry.

And the jigsaws are together with borders and all,

And they're stuck on the wall which you find is too tall,

For the massive great puzzle you bought in a sale

Of a giant whale sounding and the length of its tail.

When you've read all the books on shelf and on floor,

When there's nothing on telly that isn't a bore,

When no one calls round and you've nothing to say

And returning to bed doesn't even hold sway.

Well this was the situ in which found the Grumpete

As he sat on his bum-burned and tousled old seat.

He was bored as a bored thing can possibly get

Without smoking a pipe or unhealthy cig'rette.

He paced up and down and scratched of his gob,

And picked of his nose and disposed with a lob.

But what was the reason for this lack of get go?

I'll tell you right now, so as not to be slow.

For the Kazza Princess was not from this land

To which Grumpete her took when offering his hand.

And oft times she dreamed of returning to see

Her disdainful parents and strange family

Who had thought ill of her choice in choosing the Grump

Who they thought was an uncouth, stink-filled, sweaty

lump.

The result of this view was that she went all alone,

While the Grump stayed back without her in their home.

Before the days of the Kazz it was easy to find

Pastimes and hobbies if he had a mind.

He could always find things to scratch and to do,

Even if it just was being adrift on the loo

And floating about for a while in the bay
Entertaining himself where the poofishes play.

But since his entwinement romantic did start
He had lost for himself the self-entertain art.
Not even King Louis could he find with to play
For KL had himself gone off and away.
A teenager has friends and a need for a team
And to be all alone and to sit and to dream,

So 'twas with the King, he had gone for a week,
So his pubescent company wasn't there to be seek.
Which left just Grumpete in the house near the shore,
Being bored in the way I've described of before.
So there's only one thing that can hap in this case;
It's to do with the larder, the fridge and the face.
Yes, into the kitchen the Grumpete wund his way,
As the lengthening hours made a week of the day.
He stared at the fridge and thought what was inside.
Only one way to know, so the handle he tried.

THE THINKER

The door swung right open and sure he did gape

At the stacked pots and plates and bowls every shape.

They sat and they beckoned, "Come eat some of me,

It's hours after lunch and hours before tea.

Just a wee bite or nibble or mouthful or two,

A nothing, a morsel, just one sock or one shoe."

The Grumpete he thought as this thought did arise,

That he had a rumble of gut and a lust in his eyes.

So he reached out a hand and took of a tart,

Which he stuffed in his gob. It was just the start.

After that had gone down, he reached in again

And extracted a mousse of poached-eggified hen,

Which glistened with juices and remains of an egg

Coagulate by a half-eaten leg.

It was but short work to make of this dish

Before he looked up to ponder his stomach's next wish.

A jellying beanfest, a running sock pie,

A salvo of puddings which he threw to the sky

And swallowed right down with gusto and skill

And roared his delight over beach and down hill.

He was no longer bored and he hoped for to aid

The room in the fridge which his snacking had made.

So down went a nugget of twice gargled prune

And a green-festered cheese like a sickening moon.

And when that was gone, he proceeded to lift

Up a casserole's lid and gave it short-shrift.

With one shelf to go, he let go a belch,

Then guzzled right down a fresh bowl of welks.

A medley of veggies, a sack of ice cream,

A tunnock of beef which had burst at the seam.

He picked out the last crumb with a skilful long finger,

Til done with the fridge there was no need to linger.

For turning around he thought what could be harder

Than having a peek inside their giant larder.

His stomach was stretching now and had some more

space

And directed his brain to fill the hole in his face

With whate'er it could find in the invitesome pantry

Which stretched really far like a long warehouse gantry.

The food was stacked long, the food was stacked high.

It was ready and waiting, he didn't know why

He'd not thought of before to eat of this trove.
So forwards his frame begunned it to move.

A dried sack of giblets went into the maw
Espied by the eyes and retrieved by the paw,
And deposited fast into Grumpeter's grand gullet,
Leaving of no time to ponder or mull it.

With that done, some jars full of condiment stew
Were lost out of sight in the great noisome brew
Which churgled and gurgled all out of the sight
Of anyone watching, if watchers there might.

But you'll know it's not poss to eat of so much
Without changes to weight, and to shape, size and such.
And so was it here as the food piled on in,
That his body made space and condemned not the sin.
Sure it made farts and churned once in a while,
But it was in cahoots and that was its style
Of going along with the Grumpete's largesse
To himself at the least as he ripped off his vest
Which was starting to shrink, it appeared of to him.
Then from a large carcass he ripped off a limb.

Next came four packets of pigwhisker biscuits,

Although past their use-by he decided to risk it,

And gobbled them down with nary a care

Before turning his mind to voluminous fare.

A skillet of bugdrops, a bushel of toast

Went down at a speed which would lead to a boast

In one not so given to just getting on

With the thing upon which he had started upon.

Some boxes of fillings he dispatched with great zeal,

Then looked around more for the next stage of the meal.

In turning he bonked of his gut on the frame

Of the door while he swallowed some hangings of game.

He swallowed it whole and chewed with his throat

So his teeth could starting chewing on spare ribs of goat,

And the non spare ones too which had once round

                                        encased

The particular organs with which a pie was now laced.

He fetched of a chair for his legs they were struggling

To hold up his weight and had begun to go wuggling.

He flopped on a stool and was surprised by a creak,
Then a crash as some stool-smashing havoc was wreak.
It could not withstand the weight of the belly
Distended right now and a-wobbling like jelly.

He bulged and he prodded but pulled himself up
And a flagon of soup commenced of to sup,
While dipping the while of great hunks of bread
The size of a hippopotamus's head.

That done, he reached out for the next thing to munch,
While his tummy's insides 'gan to stir and to crunch.
Suety cakes and barrels of fruit
Fell down the well of his mouth in pursuit
Of the marzipan slice and the candystodge fudge
Which lodged midst the pile and refuséd to budge.

A sack of bright turnip, a bale of kale,
A sirloin once cut from a large passing whale.
At last the Grumpete thought perhaps he should stop -
Just after the flagon of barley and hop.
Besides that his gut was beginning to groan:
In a metaphorical sense to reach for the phone

And dial 999 for emergency services,

For food had filled up all the last of his crevices.

Yet then the Grump's eyes alighted upon

A marvellous, sumptuous mound of a scone.

It went in his gob and he started to chew.

There was nothing more now that his body could do.

He was bloated and huge like an inhaling whale,

His tightly stretched skin was greying and pale.

The sweat on his brow stood out like the dew

And his eyes were a-watering, obscuring his view.

The scone rumbled down like a slow-moving tank,

Shouldering foodstuffs and forming in rank,

And squeezing it all where no squeezing was left,

For of space or stretchroom he was completely bereft.

He shuddered, he snorted, his bottom went "phip!"

And down on the floor he started to slip.

But before he touched down on his carpet outmoded,

The mighty Grumpete's gut simply exploded.

It wasn't the sound (a wild whooshing roar)

Which remained in his memory like a top ranking score;

It wasn't the erupting rainbow of colour

As the foodstuffs rushed out one after the other;

But rather the sudden relief and absence of torsion

That came straight on after the gruesome explorsion.

So there he sat dazed, completely surrounded

By the victual battlefield, some digested and rounded.

While below his chest was a raggedy hole:

It was clear that his boredom had taken a toll.

But what to do now, the kitchen was a sight.

The Kazz would be cross, he did not want a fight.

So he folded his skinflaps 'cross the gape of his gut

And stopped it from recklessly flapping about,

While he wandered in search of a thing for to bind

His tum parts together and tie it behind.

He found gaffer tape and wrapped it around

Himself time after time til he was tightly bound.

Then out of the broom cupboard he took bucket and

spade

And set off to clean up the mess that he'd made.

It took solid hours to shovel it up,

And other ones too for the cupboards to wup.

Each bucket of fodder he tipped into containers,

For he and the Kazz were great entertainers.

For inside his tract it had hardly had time

To decompose much or be turned into chyme,

Which is what's left of your groceries got by duodenum

After gastric secretion by the tummy has seen 'em .

A few long days later the Kazza returned,

And kissed on the cheek he for who her heart burned.

While our hero looked up with a whiskery grin

And patted a belly still looking quite thin.

"Have you been busy?" she asked of to him.

He replied "It's amazing what I could pack in."

Enjoy this book?
You can make a big difference

For independent authors, honest reviews are a powerful way of bringing their books to the attention of other readers.

If you've enjoyed this book, I'd be very grateful if you could spend a few minutes leaving a review (it can be as short as you like) at your favourite online retailer.

About the author

Find out more about Kevin Barron at www.kabarron.com.

For the even more digitally minded, you can also connect with him on Twitter at @kabarronauthor, on Facebook at www.facebook.com/kabarronbooks and if you feel like it, send him an email at kevin@kabarron.com.

Also by Kevin Barron

Travel and humour

Into the blue

Half-planned travels of an amateur vagabond

Kevin feels guilty if he stays at home and does nothing. His solution is to visit other countries and do nothing there instead. An added benefit is that writing about it gives him something to do at home.

Lose your ticket before you've even set off, find out what whalers think of Greenpeace, dodge dive-bombers, meet dangerous truckers, interview a tennis star, witness horror, walk all night, fish for your dinner, watch sunsets in the wilderness, ride legendary highways, stargaze in the Rockies, hitch-hike through the outback, be rescued by an angel, become Robin Hood, escape from Colditz.

This collection of stories covers more than a decade of travel, so throw your backpack over your shoulder and head off...into the blue.

Not there yet

Wandering home with an amateur vagabond

When you leave, at what point do you start going home? And when you leave and don't come back, where is home?

Moving to another country for a while provides an excellent opportunity to travel on the way. Having threatened The Big Trip for years, Kevin finally takes the plunge and, as a result, finds that the idea of home is not as clear as it used to be.

Kayak in the rain, meet an Aboriginal elder, make conversation with a grumpy barber, kill sheep, crash a car, eat entrails, be in the Middle East on 9/11, ride legendary highways, find yourself face to face with an elk, get lost in the African night, have the best view at Shangri-La, fight a fire, be ill on an overnight bus, search for intruders, flirt, haggle, dance, joke, eat, hike, misunderstand, leave home and return.

This collection of stories follows those of *Into the blue*, so throw your backpack over your shoulder again and set off on the never ending journey home.

Light Funnel

**A father in despair. An ancient destiny.
A darkness that can change everything.**

Nothing has been right for Charlie since his father, Richard, lost his job and became depressed. When Richard disappears completely, strange dreams and visions that have been haunting Charlie lead him to a world whose inhabitants can conjure beings of light.

Meanwhile Richard has also fallen between the worlds and now finds himself amongst descendants of lost crusaders called the Order, who are facing a decisive conflict with an ancient enemy.

A discovery has been made which will overturn the balance of power. The forces of the Order are marching, but what Richard does not realise is that the enemy are sheltering his own son.

As darkness pours from the earth and armies gather, Richard and Charlie will face the nightmare from a lost past which threatens to consume both worlds.

They must find each other, and escape the approaching storm, if they are to have any hope of staying alive or returning home again.

Light Needle

In dreams, something is stirring.

Eight years have passed since the events described in *Light Funnel*.
An uneasy peace has existed between the Order and the Delf. Now,
rumblings of dissent threaten a return to war.

Inspired by dreams, Jack Silver searches for the descendants of
the adventurers who left Outreterre centuries before and never
returned. With their help, the Delf could be overthrown forever.

Former adversaries Berwick, Rodon and Raul secretly follow
Silver and his protectors across the sea; Solimo, still haunted by his
experiences, is about to face his greatest fear, while a footloose
Charlie Denham will soon be fleeing for his life from forces he does
not understand.

For an old enemy has found a way out of Limbo and will stop at
nothing to purge the worlds.

When he returns, a great city will burn and a society will be torn
apart. Only a fragile web of alliances, old and new, stands before the
terrible new power emerging from Limbo.

In this second book in the *Light Funnel* series, multiple storylines
weave together culminating in a climactic confrontation.

Later books in the series will be:

> *Light Cradle*
> *Light Mage*

Business

How to Run Facilitated Workshops
A pragmatic guide to successful meetings

Are your meetings a waste of time?
Get productive.

We've all had those moments when you wonder what the point is of getting together at work. People wander off topic, take over, tune out...

In today's fast-moving business environment, you need to make the most of people's time, energy and knowledge.

The book is aimed at business users who have limited time and budget to achieve their objectives, but wish to do so in as inclusive, consultative, yet efficient a way as possible.

It provides pragmatic advice of immediate use to both novice and practising facilitator. It can be read end to end, or you can dip into it depending on your need.

This book is packed full of advice and techniques to help you prepare for, run and follow up on facilitated workshops. Not only is the process described, but there is advice for dealing with problems along the way, notably managing behaviour that can kill productivity and collaboration. There is a focus on planning the workshop and setting out the agenda. A set of sample agendas covering a wide range of project scenarios is included.

With the advice in this book, gleaned from twenty years of experience in industry and consulting, you can pre-empt problems and be well on the way to saving time and achieving usable outcomes that will accelerate your projects.

Assuming you can believe it after reading the book you're holding in your hand, Kevin Barron has worked in industry and consulting for more than 25 years. He has led teams, worked on projects and delivered training across many sectors including banking, media, retail, wealth management, telecommunications, transport, IT services, utilities, local and national government, and manufacturing. He has facilitated hundreds of workshops in the UK, Australia, New Zealand, Sweden and Germany. He is also an experienced business analyst and agile practitioner and a popular presenter.

www.ingramcontent.com/pod-product-compliance
Lightning Source LLC
Chambersburg PA
CBHW060652030426
42337CB00017B/2581